Harriet Tarlo

Also by Harriet Tarlo:

Poetry:

Sleight of Foot (with Miles Champion, Helen Kidd and Scott Thurston)
                (Reality Street Editions, London, 1996)
Brancepeth Beck (The Other Press, London, 1997)
Love/Land (rem•press, Cambridge, 2003)
Nab (Etruscan Books, Buckfastleigh – forthcoming, 2005)

Harriet Tarlo

Poems 1990-2003

Shearsman Books
Exeter

First published in the United Kingdom in 2004 by
Shearsman Books Ltd
58 Velwell Road
Exeter EX4 4LD

http://www.shearsman.com/

ISBN 0-907562-45-0

Copyright © Harriet Tarlo, 2004.
The right of Harriet Tarlo to be identified as the author of this work has been asserted by her in accordance with the Copyrights, Designs and Patents Act of 1988. All rights reserved. No part of this publication may be reproduced, stored in a retrieval system, transmitted in any form or by any means, electronic, mechanical, photocopying, recording or otherwise, without the prior permission of the publisher.

Front cover illustration:
Out of Summer I, oil on canvas, 168 x 117cm., 2001, by Julia Ball.
Reproduced by permission of the artist.
Copyright © Julia Ball, 2001.

Acknowledgements

Some of these poems have appeared before in *Oasis*; *Talisman*; *Subvoicive Poetry*; *Gard du Nord*; *Jacket*; *Poetry Quarterly Review* and *Sleight of Foot*, RSE 4packs: No.1, Reality Street Editions, 1996. Many thanks to the editors of these publications.

Thanks are also due to supporters of the work, past and present, and those to whom poems are dedicated: Julia Ball, Sean Breadin, Richard Caddel, Thor Ewing, Frances Presley, and Simon Ross.

CONTENTS

Writing Outside
— short poems   7

my self   9
open / the back door   10
flass vale   11
emergence   12
Puyé   13
weardale   14
blue blue blue   15
off the M6   16
mid-November   18
pulling through   19
may   20
mid-may through june   21
wanting to achieve   22
throwing / away   23
slow riddles   24
shelter radio   25
beck's running after   26
not seeing the result   27
windowpanes   28
well it's better than all't rain in't it   29
just April   30
early words   31
from the rain   32
Closed for Ripening   33

Voices
— short poems   35

distance / is required   37
summer   38
air and grass in water   39
telephone?   40
Roger's poem   41
when's the train pet?   42
betrayal is betrayal   43
rains   44
I must go now   45
in Whitley Bay   46
door   47
the Englishman's fridge in Japan   48
lane to lane   49
coloured pictures   50
sunday train   51
in the freemarket nineties...   53
Arizona 2001   54
something she wants   55
away   56
running machine   57

Roads and Weather
— short sequences   59

life by fire   61
Improvisations to Music   75
into a window   81
lost time is not living time   87
Constantine   93
Maine Coast   99
Lumley Opencast   115
Valley   129
nought-three months   137
Roads and Weather   143

I

Writing Outside

short poems

my self

a hair-hooded
shadow
over bright grass
into   twisted
bark

in eng land

```
                    open
                the back door

                                              branch
                                         top
                                    the
                               to
                          climb
                                    (singing
                                     some old hymn)



              grass
                     against grass
                       breaks
(a letter
a walnut cake
an old companionship)

                         branch
                                   against branch
                                     squeaks


                      as furniture
                          to log
                             in grate
```

flass vale

        best purple
deep
      wan
            der
                  ing
          thin
     pink

     dust
     seeds
     on green

     up
     purple
     hill
               thick

round my neck
    cold
pinkpurple sways
    touch

     eye
     wants

     down
     green
     dust

emergence

    eyes squint light-film
    against sun —
    white sea lacing
    wind catches spray
    back —
          light my eye
      wakes
    brushes aside –
    gull – sleek wet neck –
    catches her fish.

Puyé*

no time to write now
night cools round the kiva

footmarks of years
broken off where
they built
homes

and lost

* Native American Cliff Dwellings in New Mexico.

weardale

moon's gone in
fog coming
over weardale nowhere

not car not sky/fell
edge not black grass
thru snow

against
wall's stone I
fall cold into
white stream
now

                                                                        (for Julia)

blue blue blue
              sea
                        is not blue
                                               seeing in
                                               I am not
                                               eye, but

     rock
                                   air

                    light

                                     water

wind moving
       cloud
                                     rain held

                                     falling

                      water
                                           breaking
                                         shell

                       in sand
                  throwing

back
                                     light

               to moon

  waves
        over
rock

                 earth   circling

                     light

off the M6

Kendal
Windermere
      not now

grey shock of mountains

turn
fast
around
water

fog light

walls knitted grey
Newbiggin on Lune

sheep shadows falling
night through evening

Brough Sowerby
Brough

  signed to   Bowes &
                       Cotherstone

cotherstone cheese
sweetsharp milk
     almost
turn to that taste

not now

curve of bridge
    yellow

Barnard Castle

Stainton
Staindrop
Evenwood Gate

Evenwood Gate

mid-november

      turning year
white   turn off to
cotherstone   snow
after middle england
hills   always some
thing not working   my
car has no heating   no
confidence in the road   turn
     ing off to
cotherstone

    home at least some
    fire from clumsy
    kindling snapping bow
    branches   or even axe
    left lying tree working
    at warmth at home at
    something working

cold road through
to cotherstone   cracking
finger cuts rattling
each cattle grid   hurts
against white fields   why go
through whiter behind
mist double white lost any
    certain way cold

    pulling through
    me

                mud
    green water

    taste and i
    cannot

    yourself
          pulling
    against
          pull
    ing   a
    gainst

    me

may

    cold here
    even bluebells live
longer jarred
    against wallsbooks
      still –
      standing

uncrushed   trees stepp
ing hare foot   sun
   insect I   fly

out of window
into woods

mid may through june

                  hawthorn

bluebells   *may*

              rhododendron

                red campion
                    lilac
              goosegrass   *through*

              elderflower slowly

                  foxgloves
              buttercups   *june*
              clover

                    hedgerow
                    dogrose
              last flicker gorse

                odd cornflower

wanting to achieve
a round rim
a circle of experience
Duncan's meadow
I fell asleep
again and
again
all morning
to find it
and found
3 answers
forgotten
a dance
dream-life
that's real
closed again

    throwing
    away   easy

into the street
pint after pint after pint

                        or oranges
                                turning

impeding infirmities

until there's enough room
for us all

                    fresh to squeeze and cut

tape measure falling from her skirt

catching the quick way out

                    certain areas on the east coast
                    are not worth saving
                    let the sea come in

sweeping earth up
feeding it back
to the next one
shaking dead roots
free never throwing
away when the sack
breeds old hair and
blood back any
way

                        orthopaedic beds/orange
                        juice/personal loans/dead
                        geraniums

slow riddles

like
earth holding water – luminous surface –
before
         letting sink

like
the switch
when a bee quiets suddenly
— you know
         you've been listening

like
the flower husk holding traces
of purple   a space
         where petals were

   shelter radio
       sweet modulation on toast
         into stun
             slipping and

   flocks
     leaves
        turning to day, honey,
    breath's smoke

   stream, lorries, horse eating
     in sound
         sharp sorrel's seize

     we're not all doing
    every   thing
    we   said
    we   would

      so what?

beck's running after
rain
    dragging ferns in
    all those lovesick girls
       left hanging

   don't trust the sun
      water still running
        over stone & stone
         & stone

  weavers' paths
    skidding their directions
       rain needles clogs
        skitting holly leaves

   rushing iron
     hanging elderheads
        down to
      drain

not seeing the result
most of the time
     eye corners over here
  lifting
a wing until   robin ashift
from us — won't you watch
keep timing days and hours
van door slams, robin flies and
that man is looking
away   someone sees
      all of it? — it's

   not size shifting
difference — wings — light —
lift — leaving trees
  stoning life

     most of the time

windowpanes

sometimes   not quite fall
  dizzy   how you
look again   and —   behind cloud —
    spheres/branches/clouds
moving   light   another season

  ridges in glass   light
between   one   and another
spheres   not fluid

missing out connections —   [words] like "hanging
   in the balance"
              to be there
    fault in the glass line
                wearing down the pane

well it's better than all't rain in't it

February   c-rooks sawing
          beaking twigs
ice scrape   snow on the hills
bluewhite it's a fall
after a dream   "a death in
the family"   sorting through sweetmeats
what is left   over
hearing spring

                         running on ice
          a fracture
how to think   —   about the century?

                                        (for Ric Caddel)

    just April   *make opening more*
                                    natural, simpler

              thin moon in
              high window over
                    her white cot

clearing winter debris
today   thistlestick
                white out stalks
mould's greenwet

                            grass opening
                                out, drying to
                                      cut

nice use of space

        leaf leaf thru leaf

     pile of old to discard
but she's just one
and all over
it all   magpie — finding

       it's new in her month, her mouth
       earth   apple   crock
       leaf   and   biscuit
                     take the last 12 lines ... and
                     concentrate on/start from
                     there —

early words

side

                door out

home

                carrying, balancing
                        hipside

up   just   stone steps
                    each edge

                heart   missing

down   vivid sprays potsides

wet

              flagstones   lines

      clover elder sorrel
      growing between

from the rain

tarmac ruckled up
        force below/above
                earth crumple under up

falling thick into itself, excess
stone flags, steps
swim but hold

        fear falling
           arms up, stone baby
                through air in stages

thunder

           protection
           protection
           protection

                    of the soft thing

bruise from brace and balance
        holding back doors
                against knees
in from the weather
out of the rain

CLOSED FOR RIPENING

strawberries in Yorkshire

        a girl's circle

    round   in which

        she

  holds

a few words

when one is lost, one lives

pulling, worrying at skin

      making salad, waiting

for the guests

      it's not a one trick story

II

Voices

short poems

    distance
    is required

sorrysorryohsosorry
on the telephone
looking   out of the window
past the   folded back
        curtain

onto the street.

    a telephone
    a window
    a curtain
    a street

    dis   tance
    is required

    cer tain ly

summer

not another sound from you tonight —
goodnight.

mam turn on the dark will you?

air and grass in water

the newspaper is the traditional refuge
of the fathers

a flock of cows
flock of cows
a flock
black and white
white and black

    air and grass in water

and the river turned blue
    under
      sun
traditionally red
              blue   red
              red   blue

    which are you?

telephone?

bird high call
high

green light
sun
lights

man hits nails
on stone
shooting practice?

home   [*go to sleep now*]
yellow curtains
and I did not
   hear

soft soft soft
of   [something swallowing?]

is it pigeons?

Roger's poem

only one
mind's colour
picture
heightened by you –
not known –
now dead

lean
back
    eye sunwet

"brace yourself"
and faster than the sail
    whips the wind you've
crossed – a big man –
                           your bright boat.

when's the train pet?

when's the train pet? any train
I'm not going anywhere
I want to take a photograph
10 minutes, that's good
I'll stand here I think
seems the right spot

    blue fur hat
    over peaked cap
    over specs
    on nose
    over
    grin
    (teeth missing)

    a green dress

    standing in
    trainers
    in her right spot
    camera round
    the neck

**betrayal is betrayal
wherever you may find it**

as a mother
shoots down
this girl
from her turning into
the drive wheeling
her bicycle
through
the gate
and
under the
laburnum
tree
into blood

rains

if you do that one more time I'll tell your mother
outside

rains early on
window-dirt purple

outside
filthy weather eh?

I must go now

*my son – if he gets
back
and I'm not in   then
he goes out
again*

in Whitley Bay

Spanish City

three lovers

bumping against

each edge

until they

give

        door

              wood/metal
                    key
                    turns

fumbling doorkey

             nothing to do with me

           trains
            lowfog
              blows out

       now

the Englishman's fridge in Japan

she opens
his fridge

look, look
he said *what-more-do-you-want?*
> *look at all the food*
> *I've bought for you*

he thinks it's food I want
I can't eat anyway

when he goes home
to England
he'll buy me food
to stay

    lane to lane
        keeping speed
            under the sun

you lean into me
        the paper's corner
            across my vision

your voice in my
        body – striking pictures – as I
            shift the wheel, hold

the pedal down and
      glide,   your
            head a hieroglyph

dead centre, against flashing
      cars   still
          as we pass

later – you take the back seat –
and lean
back   on the parcel shelf
            eyes closed

        neck
            stretched
                out
I see your whole
        body, thrown back,

        glistening

coloured pictures

squares of colour
        shading, rubs paper
                      museum labels
              the past, the child's
        names   hold

space spread
origami wings folding,
        unfolding

                the adult's drafting eye
                knowing

                taking time

in pink and blue and green
getting it right
                hand shading
                wanting
                beauty from

reflecting squares
of colour on paper, once
under her
touch

        her feet
            as she runs

sunday train

sweet food   rich yet light
pulls apart
                like tearing
                        your tears falling
                into my mouth
the way home

Peterborough
Grantham
Newark   on sticks
Retford   white plastic
Doncaster   flies wings
Wakefield
Leeds

                                scaring the birds
bird line/tail tip   just a warning
to lose
everything
you
                        I mean it's dusk
                        the gold M shines
                        bright as sun's last
                        streak
letters   people on trains
reading letters on pages
all the way home

                        can't bear each others'
                        intelligent eyeshine   or
                        judgement arrangement apologies

breaking the line

in the freemarket nineties
who can say
what a person is worth

                        honey will you
                        pass over me

let the books come up
from the floor

                        opens butterfly wings
                        to names

liking the elusive lines
(the ling)

                        without parenthesis

suggesting

                        we might

through heather burn
over until we

                        learn that we all
                        need fuel

commodities of which
you, your cells, skin,
sloes, berries, eyes
are wanted

                        your sudden shifts
                        in tone

by us without history

                        honey will I
                        pass over you?

Arizona 2001

jelly-dark shine   out of
    pale and pink and blond
        mottle   from sun element

under (flaps) thick skin
     flicks
see in?

and the elbow / knuckle / knee
joints in
angling   Americans in shorts
    hairs gilded
    dam the water
    see sun skin?

wind, ran away
       duress, duress

no mettle

something she wants

was always a part of her
life resolving around it
  taking it seriously taking
  it as read

      recedes away
each moment from her
leaving years of time
to play with

lifting her shirt up	five days old
an arm cut, hand	thin fingers, thumb
stuck under	under his fat arm
shoulder, lifting	posed, all wood, dried
up her rack	flower and quiet
of bones	places
it would not all come back	*he is rather a handsome boy*

away

off milk in rough wool
& the smile, that smile
then that cry

    softest then the lips
    as they mutate
    shape, shape
        in   round square,

            knit   underpin
            in that wool
                imprint
                    in-print
                    knit thru

running machine

turning our cloth

viscose cotton polyester fleece

silk turn words round

each other and round

other in argument – new clothes

for old, when old

would do

as we only know know know

they would

III

Roads and Weather

short sequences

life by fire

living by fire only

stone never

gives in

to fire   warmth a few feet

                       around

             me   around

cold walls

cold glass

                family at home
  reading beside coal   past
  trying
  to keep our
  distances equal

   damp black coal shone
   smoked thickly

   bringing in snow

       walking –

  breathing coal – thru

    winter villages

  Bowburn, Langley

miners' relics

wood falls free   trees

dying tangling

            in living

branches   fall

ready

      count yourself lucky

I save the piece of coal

that falls through

the grate-hole

rich black jewel

    burning eyes staring

          beside

fire

    wind changing   smoke

    choking   waiting

    wood screeching too wet

    bleeding yew

    loudly

    sweet wood burns out blood

    in the grate

**Wednesday 16 January to
Thursday 17 January 1991**

finally

and fire lights

and sheep dog

    barks

cars almost audible

    finally

        we cross

kindling smells like chocolate
drying quickly stacked
neatly

to spark
      any kind of tree

blazes when
war kindles out of
      kin and kin

who is not of my kind
who is not kind

only smaller sticks of wood
for kindling   sap
drying
out

I blend hawthorn
> with fircone

> yew with

> elder

> oak

> and alder

changes light

today flames

white in dusty sunflake

flecks plant dying silver

casting shadows

light dust against

white

cracks in wood

slowly warming

for next winter

I went alone

into

wood

no one

saw me

carried it back

and burnt it

lying to sleep

fire fell into

its own

hollow

down

to grey

coal tastes

like comfort

on finger

 pulling

  down

called to account

a talent (a sheep, a goat?)

long enough you've had

    sitting

counting cones burn

on the cold floor

Improvisations to Music

Mignon
for Amy

      voice
         string
bow   stone   takes
    to air

    finger bone
      plucks

and back bends
    over air

  song
  into
  water

Crwth

    strains air
heart's throat pulls
take grassbeat
crwth
     croaning into
   strain grass heart
     crwth
  through
      under
      voice
   under
   strings
under
earth

crwth down -
pulling

recorder, gemshorn, crwth,
  lute and bones

catches
   from to from
to fall
   settle & catch
 sweet & sickle
   low & call
  bone
    slail
fasten
hill-all   to
   pull

Hungarian field recordings
for Sean

       fire beat
       b/air wood beat
       en dark/fair
       red play
       hands on wood
       beat fire
       fl/airs

into a window

rain
pollen
petal

blood dance

after sun

rooks   circle
windows
riding new winds

trees meet secret
seeming

there isn't any angle
for seeing
leaf branch   branch
leaf inter-sect

flat I see green
summer - wanting
to step up
from white elder
down
from high white
window
into
trees   inside
almost sap into
vein of leaf gold
essence of green
before sun meets
creeping tree
into tree into
tree

green sky
was winter road /
house / farm /
opencast

now   into a window
thin rain   and red
leaves twisting back
to green
in stony window
framed behind
bottles / plants / dead
still leaf
silhouettes from
under grey light bulb
as sun
leaves
day

lost time is not living time

green time
scarred alive
under bedground
six months unliving time
lost

green window
quiet under
bedground
watching
not living
time

gold line
white line
grey slate

barnacles
indenting feet

she runs with her
head up

i know
it's the right thing

the green grey stone
the green grey stone
the green grey slate
the white gold quartz

black tar
green weed
sea

I would have known
you
I would have entered
you   like the sea
her low slate pools
wearing your sweet
surface away
to the quartz bone
through tangled weed
under
                  cold stone

Constantine

going out
  over
  cliff-fields
        looking
  back,
  inland streams stream
  down to
  sea

   up at clouds over
   me, back at
   bay's long steep
   fall to
   sea

in-land
bird-circling village

    where's old
Constantine (church and well
mapped on my paper)?

   narrow
   paths re
   turn me to
   dunes and
   sea

where's old Constantine (church and well
mapped on my paper

   the old church – what
   on the golf course you mean? no
   you can't find it with the map

   go back to the course – you've
   got to be careful mind – lie flat if they
   shout at you –

> *and where the stream*
> *runs parallel – no, not parallel, across the*
> *course, strike off on the rough to your*
> *left*
>
> *it's the 4th hole on the short course – once*
> *you've found that, you're there – climb the*
> *hill and it's in the dip below –*
> *it's only a few stones mind, but*
> *I like it*

Constantine (church and well)   hidden
behind sculpted
golf slopes, dips, hills,
grass covering streams that could
place you

worn track, arched door, three walls
falling

in your wall, niches
for sacrament or cross –
ivy over you – ivy
grows over your walls –
ivy hides you down
to earth

      ground

      only arch stays stone against
      ivy, green bramble,
      grass, against
      celandine

                                boy plays 4th hole (does
                                not see)
                                boy's brother plays
                                4th hole (does not see)
                                mother, father play 4th
                                hole (do not see)

                Constantine

        its own green
        memory,
        unsigned, unclimbed

        below, between two streams,
        the well, roofed to
        keep golf balls out

did they walk from scant homes over
low wet land, to
water between stone walls
under stone, in cool dankness, feet
slipping to gather
water, fresh her, falling
down to
sea?

                                you walked in,
                                drew water,
                                talking or
                                silent,
                                listening,
                                resting
                                shawl or butter or
                                milk from

                    the farm
                    in the niche
                    to stay dry

                    inside
                    low well
                    constantine

          hearing waves on rocks

church and well, well
and church
over grey over
green and
down to
sea

Maine Coast

> WELCOME TO MAINE
> THE WAY LIFE SHOULD BE

Portland
hot tar after
hurricane
cedar-slatted
edges cool green
cats move between

Casco Bay
once
"the Resting Place of the Great Blue Heron"

take the diamond trail boat trail!
see Great Diamond Island/
Great White Houses/Great Blue swimming pools!
once "Hog Island"
 pigs lived here

                far out
                Russian fish-canning ship
                anchors all summer– rusty, red

                – birds
                wild for fish
                flying
                the fiddle –

                3 burnt red men almost
                naked stop
                dead to
                watch

                nothing happens

                – birds
                wild for fish
                fly out
                the fiddle –

route one
looking for shoreline

| PRIVATE LAND |

| PRIVATE LAND |

| PRIVATE LAND |

                    shoreline   finding

                    sandpipers fast
                    hunting at sea's shifting
                            edging
                  fine
                  line

            finding   shoreline

PEMAQUID BEACH STATE PARK
BEACH RULES

NOT ALLOWED ON THIS BEACH
BOATING   OPEN FIRES
VEHICLES   LITTERING
PETS ALCOHOLIC BEVERAGES

PLEASE KEEP OFF THE DUNES

Have A great DAY!

Restrooms CLOSE AT 5:00pm
GATES LOCKED AT 7:00pm

South Bristol

the draw bridge up
a postcard
– the first one –
paint-peeled boats,
sun on wet
lobster pots

Mount Desert
(once Pemeteq)

1604, the French found it (*Isle de Monts Desert*)
then the English (*Arcadia*)
  the Hudson River painters
     the buyers of bird feathers
        for ladies' hats

the Penobscots gave it up
to the State of Massachussets
then sold
birds to milliners
  canoes to sportsmen
     baskets to tourists

and finally themselves
in early pale
photographs:
Indian family at Bar Harbour
(once Man-es-ayd'ik
 "clan gathering
place")

now a national park where
you can't pick a stone
or sea lavender
for luck

    the Penebscot Indian Nation
    – population 2000 –
    is up the river now
    at Old Town
    selling audio cassettes
    and bingo tickets
    its high stakes

Seawall

stone bar holds ocean
back
from low
land

fog

dark drops on stone
   water
       changes
  rain as tide

light – nothing to see –
 bells
calm and hear nothing

dark drops on stone

only seaweed stays
the same
in rain

and seawall dining room
at night

haven't seen the sea all day
– this fog –
she says

taking up her fork
to scratch her back

Wendell Gilley Museum
(plumber, then bird-carver,
Southwest Harbour, Maine)

Wendell Gilley's hands
tapping a finished bird
gently

soothing it for the camera

grey knuckles – loose
from carving

> *mekin' birds –*
> *gave up plumbin' in the end*
> *for it*
> *put my son through college*
> *on it*
> *in just one lifetime you*
> *couldn't begin to*
> *grasp it*

> *never did get one to suit me*

Wendell Gilley's first bird (1930)
basswood mallard drake
dark, shiny
solid – decoy,
sitting duck

> *as you get older you just get to the point*
> *where there's no desire to shoot at all*

       his later birds
might move, painted feathers
shifting – painted eye
glinting   as
close as can be
to what you see

> *just common birds, just common ducks,*
> *not many hawks – a few hawks –*
> *a lot of owls, a lot of owls*

later, outside   that cormorant
still under rain
wings raised

could take wood in my hand, a knife,
> *whittle off a little here*
> *and a little there*

could sit here all day
> *happy as a fool*

wonderland

rained cobwebs
      asters

pine gives
way to
salt

shore mist

is it birds or
rock tips?

Cranberry Isles

Little Cranberry

where roads run out to the sea's clear edge
from
grey sand   across
to fine slipping pebbles
on Gilley Beach

where they dried fish
sent ice to the
Carribean

where Mary Ann Carroll
tried to break free
from her family by
teaching children
saved up
put her money
in a boat –
lost it at sea

where   the Great Blue Heron
took off
awkwardly
from
Middle Pond

Great Cranberry

from mudflats and weed   across
to great pinkish clambering
stones

    on Dog Point Lane
grasshoppers leap
and fall
leap and fall
on their sides, their fronts
their backs
    right themselves and
leap and fall
again

Great Pond, Mt Desert

waterwindlap
after walking

stone
southside

cormoront swims out
beneath feet
      side to
side   watching

waterwindlap
after walking

birds' wings
loud   oversound
as walking feet to them,
      flying
overwater

no one about
cool, almost fall

expecting vistas

seeing
only
trees

Back on Route 1

> **STOP FOR
> BREAKFAST AND LUNCH**
> if you don't, we'll both starve!

Lumley Opencast

last day

on past diversion signs
same fieldpaths
same hedgerows
smoky fireweed
dies back
again

diggers
from four sides
draw quiet earth-lines
diagonal through stubble

roll up roaring
shatter buried
china, buried
bottles
shine
dark morning

blasting

    red flag
    stone breaks/ thrown
    up to mock cairns

    was it always there?
    under earth
        crop
        sky
        crust

    holding us up

crane

(after seeing Kandinsky)

steel crane

yellow horse
and rider over
the hill of opencast

lost walks

rains 8.00 a.m.
postmistress's dog
sulks on her lead

eyes edge to
wild ground

jealousy

lost names

my wife was born in Lumley
lived here all her life

knew it when there were more pubs
than houses

and the names of every field
lived on a farm as a bairn
you see

glad she didn't live to see this
all the new houses

now this

lost circle

woods, river, fields
fields, river, woods

woods, river
    river, woods

part of the circle's gone

lost perspective

used to lie in bed
in summer

look over the fields
to Lumley

till me Dad called me
down

never look out of that window now

summer

strange grasses
grow and
open
wide to mocking
poppy heads

open/close
the shutter on
old cornfields

closer eye

under poppies
bold statement
fields edge old
sentiment:

vetch
chickweed
yellow mustard
and (no poetic license)
forget-me-not

primary days

man in red shirt
stops blue car
to photograph
the poppy wall
of opencast

brilliant picture
he is and
takes

primary days

lost

hedgerows
trees
wasteland

paths through

Valley

(Morton Woods, Holme Valley)

August

goldfinch flits the lane
to the valley

soles' clap tarmac, limbs
surprising shake
down

bluebell husks
earth colour now
flower

spreading yellow is

October   beech leaves falling slow

like snow starting   but gold   bright weight filling out
                                    ground

scuffed no use boots
trying to feel through   light
throws water shadows onto
ferns ripple
move

holly seedlings take hold
through Autumn

CLOSED
DUE TO FLOODING

ravages of nature
these great floods
news reporters getting biblical

                footpath falling bridge
         over stepping stone
              covered green   still
    growing under
        water   luminous lost

April

sycamores
pink (wrapped) fat buds
pale power succulence
(furled)
behind leaf serration bronze
red zig
zag

saxifrage sticks yellow tips/stamens out
bright of green rock cover

come now spring insects

June

sorrel reds over buttercups

dark down valley
dense   bluebells fading pale over
sodden green mud leaves

hearsong blackbird, chaffinch
goldfinch unseen
squeak

nought-three months

    raising eyebrows curiously   dark eye opens
         and shuts
                        seeing no-thing
    turning   turning   to side
wide open   mouth   pull and fill
pull and fill
        and close

                              fast warm
                  thru her nose   breath
                  and breath and breath
                  oh
                  it it oh?

stretch   it's a stretching at edges
        hard ends bed
leg edge
push kick

              arms flung back and up
                    let go
            in sleep, sleep   mouth
              still dream-suckling

                                eyes   turn to the
                    light   seeing
                under trees
                                    leaf-flux
                            flicker it's
                    mo ving

        reaching   grasp out it

and hold   colour shape in space
take space up
and out it
want

                        pulls hairstrands out
                                winding round fingers
            into mouth

                                focus and shine   light
                                    open   wide
                                        wide
                                    eye   mouth
                                    world bite

    arms   held out in sleep
                      balancing
        float down
steady close

                panic flutter
                      stare out and wide-eye
                                it's alright

                hairy shadows hang over
                      her, holding   keep sun away
          secret mind
                            soft under fontanelles
                skin, something
                    mo ving

Roads and Weather

Cowcliff Hill Road
warm in november

gorse, sorrel, bilberry
open to weather   flowering whatever

Clough Foot Lane

fields on one side, sheep,

plantation

on the other   conifers for what?

Greave Road

guard dog outside the egg farm

barks, chickens sqwawks chained

up on concrete

cars riding past their smell

too fast

        calves' ears

flapping

Sike Lane

starts under stone

going to grass

April

turning to earth

then mud

looking over Wooldale

      to Castle Hill

      angle

      all the little houses

      slip

      away

      down valley

Scholes Moor Road

July, 3 days sun

mowing mowing hay catching

throat and nose

red poppies, white clover

all along hedgerows

Good King Henry on Bent Lane, little

to change

bilberries by lower Longley cottages

    teasels at the corner   stone slates on the

        roof   older, older   and names, yarrow

            scaring larks in the field

                kestrel parallel over the heather

Ryecroft Lane

to Hade Edge, August

between two walls

        pappus and dust

cows got in the playground　　　*no?!*

walls fall up

Printed in the United Kingdom
by Lightning Source UK Ltd.
130422UK00001B/260/A